Learning Musical Instruments

Should I Play the
Flute?

Nicola Barber

Heinemann
LIBRARY

www.heinemann.co.uk/library
Visit our website to find out more information about Heinemann Library books.

To order:
 Phone 44 (0) 1865 888066
 Send a fax to 44 (0) 1865 314091
 Visit the Heinemann Bookshop at www.heinemann.co.uk/library to browse our catalogue and order online.

First published in Great Britain by Heinemann, Halley Court, Jordan Hill, Oxford, OX2 8EJ, part of Harcourt Education.

Editorial: Nancy Dickmann and Sarah Chappelow
Design: Richard Parker and Manhattan Design
Picture Research: Melissa Allison and Natalie Gray
Production: Camilla Crask
Illustrations: Jeff Edwards
Originated by Modern Age
Printed and bound in China by Leo Paper Group

The publishers would like to thank Teryl Dobbs for her assistance in the preparation of this book.

The author would like to thank Joanne Boddington for her invaluable help in the preparation of this book.

10 digit ISBN 0 431 05785 0
13 digit ISBN 978 0431 05785 9

11 10 09 08 07
10 9 8 7 6 5 4 3 2 1

British Library Cataloguing in Publication Data
Barber, Nicola
Should I learn to play the flute?. - (Learning musical instruments)
1.Flute - Juvenile literature 2.Flute music - Juvenile literature
I.Title
788.3'2

Acknowledgements
The publishers would like to thank the following for permission to reproduce photographs: Christie's Images Ltd p. **7**; Corbis pp. **5** (Ariel Skelley), **15** (Lindsay Hebberd), **16** (Albrecht G. Schaefer), **17** (Tiziana and Gianni Baldizzone), **20** (Reuters); Getty Images p. **23** (AFP); Harcourt Education Ltd/Tudor Photography pp. **8**, **9**, **12**, **13**, **24**, **25**, **26**, **27**; Library of Congress p. **9**; PhotoEdit p. **18** (James Shaffer); Rex Features p. **10** (Peter De Voecht); Robert Dick p. **22**; The Art Archive p. **6** (Dagli Orti); The Image Works p. **4** (Bob Daemmrich); Topfoto/ArenaPAL pp. **14**, **21**; UPPA p. **19** (Photoshot).

Cover image of a flautist reproduced with permission of ArenaPAL.

Contents

Any words appearing in the text in bold, **like this**, are explained in the Glossary.

Why do people play musical instruments?

Ever since early humans made simple instruments from pieces of wood or bone, people have loved to make musical noises. Music is a universal language. Everyone can enjoy making music and listening to it. Music allows people to express their feelings.

People learn to play musical instruments for many different reasons. Some want to learn a new skill. Some want to make music with other players. A few people are able to make a living from playing or teaching. Others play just for pleasure in their spare time. Best of all, music brings people together – at pop concerts, in the concert hall, or playing with friends.

Playing the flute is a very sociable activity. These flautists are marching at a band jamboree in Austin, Texas, USA.

Playing together in a wind band is fun. Players must learn to listen to each other as well as play their own lines of music.

There are thousands of different musical instruments played by people around the world. In this book you can find out about one of these instruments, the flute. The type of flute you will probably learn to play is the modern orchestral flute. This flute is part of a much bigger, worldwide family (see pages 14–17).

Why choose the flute?

You may choose to learn the flute because you love its sound, or you could choose it because of a particular piece of music you have heard. You may want to be able to play in a larger group. Examples of groups include a **wind band**, a flute choir, a marching band, or the **woodwind** section of an **orchestra**. Whatever your reasons, this book will tell you more about the flute. You will learn about its history and the people who play it.

FROM THE EXPERTS

"After 34 years of playing my instrument, it still sends a thrill down my spine to hear the sound of the flute projecting out from an orchestra..."

Joanne Boddington, professional flautist

What is a flute?

The flute is a member of a family of musical instruments that are played either by blowing down, or across, a hole at one end of a pipe. You use the fingers of both hands to cover and uncover holes along the length of the pipe to change notes.

Ancient flutes

The flute is one of the world's most ancient instruments. The oldest known flute was found in a cave in Slovenia. It dates back about 50,000 years. The flute is made from the hollow bone of a young bear and has just two **tone holes**. It is too fragile to be played. A 9,000-year-old instrument found in China is the oldest playable flute. It is made from bird bones and has seven tone holes.

This image from an Etruscan tomb in Italy dates from the 500s BC. It shows a musician performing on two flutes at the same time.

FLUTE FACTS: Different materials

Not all ancient flutes were made from bone. The ancient Greeks used **reeds** – plants with hollow stalks – to make the **panpipes**, or syrinx (see page 17 for the story behind this name). Some flutes were made from wood or bamboo. In Central and South America, people made flutes and panpipes out of clay.

Simple recorders made from wood or reed were popular across Europe for more than 300 years.

Recorders and flutes

From about 1450 until 1750 in Europe, the most popular type of flute was the **recorder**. Then the louder **transverse** ("played sideways") flute became more popular. Early transverse flutes were made from wood, with open tone holes. In the 1830s, a flautist called Theobald Boehm invented a system of levers and keys to cover the tone holes. Boehm's flute became the standard form for the modern flute.

What are flutes made from?

Most modern flutes are made from metal. However, some flautists still prefer wooden flutes. A "student" flute is the least expensive type of flute. These flutes are made from a mixture of metals. They are covered with a layer of another metal, usually silver, to protect them. Better-quality flutes are made entirely from silver. Some celebrity flautists have instruments made from solid gold or even platinum.

What are the different parts called?

The flute is made of three separate parts: the **headjoint**, **middle joint**, and **footjoint**. There are many keys.

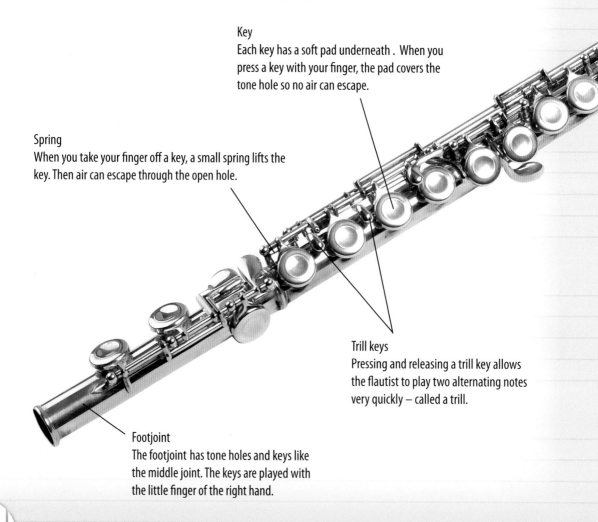

Key
Each key has a soft pad underneath . When you press a key with your finger, the pad covers the tone hole so no air can escape.

Spring
When you take your finger off a key, a small spring lifts the key. Then air can escape through the open hole.

Trill keys
Pressing and releasing a trill key allows the flautist to play two alternating notes very quickly – called a trill.

Footjoint
The footjoint has tone holes and keys like the middle joint. The keys are played with the little finger of the right hand.

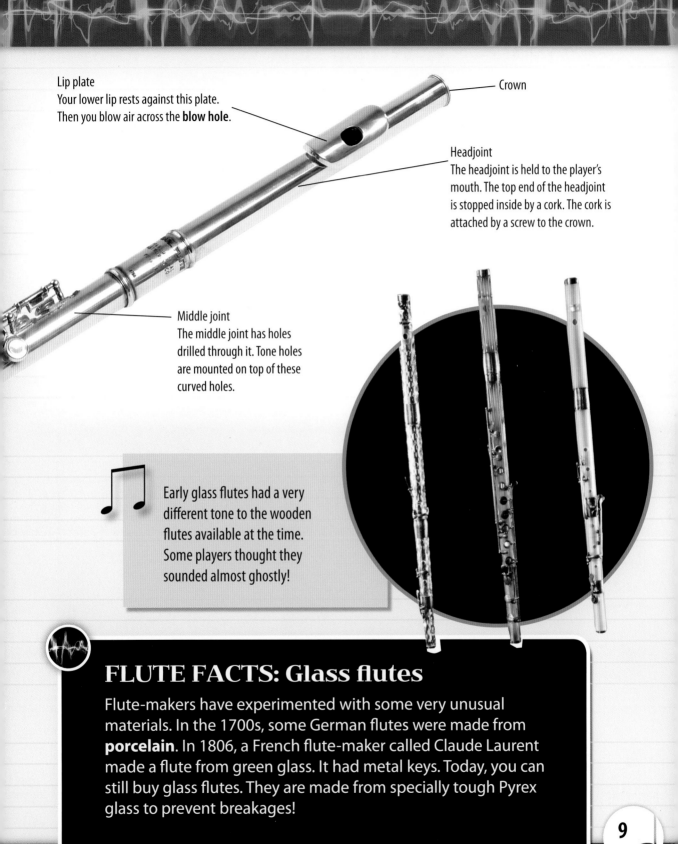

Lip plate
Your lower lip rests against this plate.
Then you blow air across the **blow hole**.

Crown

Headjoint
The headjoint is held to the player's mouth. The top end of the headjoint is stopped inside by a cork. The cork is attached by a screw to the crown.

Middle joint
The middle joint has holes drilled through it. Tone holes are mounted on top of these curved holes.

Early glass flutes had a very different tone to the wooden flutes available at the time. Some players thought they sounded almost ghostly!

FLUTE FACTS: Glass flutes

Flute-makers have experimented with some very unusual materials. In the 1700s, some German flutes were made from **porcelain**. In 1806, a French flute-maker called Claude Laurent made a flute from green glass. It had metal keys. Today, you can still buy glass flutes. They are made from specially tough Pyrex glass to prevent breakages!

How does a flute make its sound?

The flute belongs to a group of instruments called **aerophones**. These instruments produce their sound when a body of air **vibrates**. You can try making a simple aerophone by blowing across the top of a bottle. As you blow, the air inside the bottle vibrates. The vibrations make the air outside the bottle move in waves. These sound waves travel to your ears. When your ear picks up the sound waves, your brain interprets the waves as a musical note.

It takes a bit of practice to learn how to blow correctly across the blow hole to make a beautiful sound.

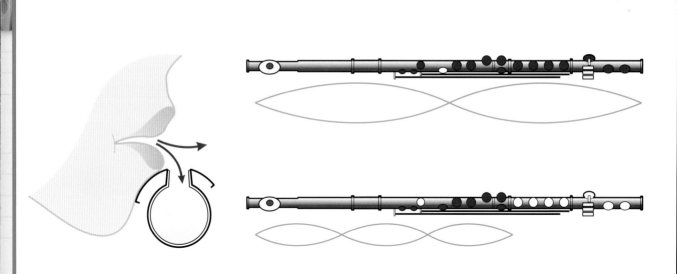

If all the holes are covered, no air can escape. The long column of air produces a low pitch. If only half the tone holes are covered, air escapes halfway down the pipe. The column of air is shorter, and the pitch higher.

High and low

The speed of these vibrations determines how high or low a note sounds. This sound is called the **pitch**. Fast vibrations produce a high pitch. Slower vibrations produce a lower pitch. There is little space for air to vibrate in a short pipe, so it vibrates quickly and produces a high pitch. There is more space in a longer pipe, so the air vibrates more slowly and produces a lower pitch. Of course, the flute is always the same length. Covering and uncovering the **tone holes** with the keys changes the length of the vibrating column of air. This alters the pitch of the note.

FLUTE FACTS: Blowing the flute

When you blow across the flute's **blow hole**, some of the air goes inside the flute. This fast-moving air starts vibrations inside the flute's body. Your ears hear these vibrations as a pitch.

How do you make a sound?

When you first try to make sound on the flute, it's a good idea to use only the **headjoint**. Hold it with both hands, with the lip plate against your bottom lip. Put the centre of your lips directly above the blow hole. It may help to look in a mirror. Now close your mouth, leaving a small opening as if you had a straw in your mouth. The shape made by your lips is called the *embouchure* (pronounced om-boo-shure), from the French word for "mouth" or "mouthpiece". This shape helps you to blow a steady stream of air across the blow hole.

You might need to adjust the position and shape of your lips before you can produce a sound. Try playing long notes, keeping your sound steady.

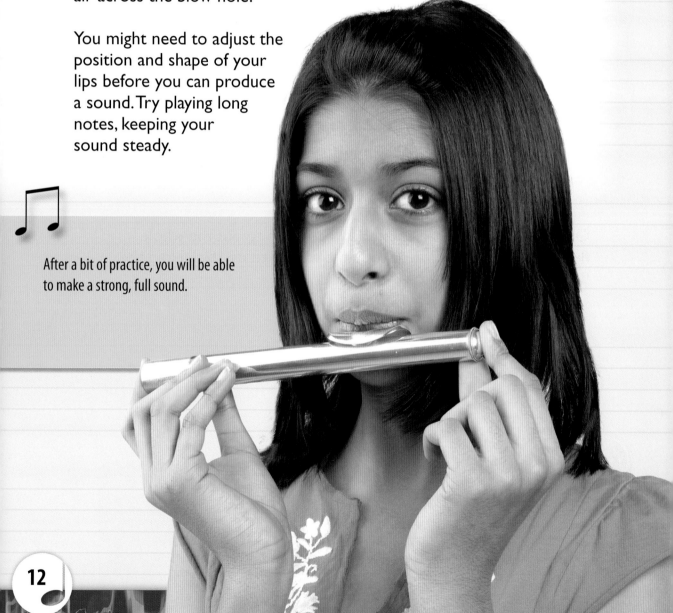

After a bit of practice, you will be able to make a strong, full sound.

You need a teacher to show you how to hold the flute properly. It's important not to pick up bad habits early on!

Where do your fingers go?

Once you can make a steady sound, it's time to put the whole flute together (see page 26 to find out how to do this). Hold the flute upright in front of you, with your left hand above your right hand. Now swivel the flute out to your right. Try sounding some long, steady notes. When you are ready, position your fingers on the keys. Hold the flute so that it is balanced between your chin, the left first finger joint and the right thumb. These three support points keep the flute steady. Your fingers and other thumb are free to work the keys. A teacher can show you how to hold your flute.

FROM THE EXPERTS

"The one who takes care in the practising of every note will be at the end a good player."

Theobald Boehm

Which musical family is the flute from?

The orchestral flute is a member of the **woodwind** family. This family also includes the flute, oboe, clarinet, saxophone, and bassoon. All of these instruments were originally made from wood. They all produce sound using a player's breath. That is why they are "wind" instruments.

Woodwind sounds

Each woodwind instrument has its own sound. The flute has a soft, gentle tone, and adds sparkle when it plays high notes. The clarinet uses a single **reed**, a thin piece of cane which fits into the clarinet mouthpiece. When the player blows, the reed **vibrates**. This gives the clarinet its velvety sound. The oboe and bassoon are double reed instruments. Their mouthpieces are made from two pieces of cane which vibrate together when the player blows. The oboe has a high, reedy sound. The bassoon has a lower, richer sound.

The woodwind section of an orchestra includes flutes, clarinets, oboes, and bassoons. The player on the left of this picture is playing a small flute, called a piccolo.

FLUTE FACTS: City of piccolos

Basel, Switzerland, is a city of piccolo players. Every year, its people celebrate Fasnacht at the beginning of the Christian festival of Lent. Masked piccolo players and drummers open the celebrations. They parade at night through dark city streets lit only by lanterns.

It is said that there are more than 10,000 piccolo players in Basel, thanks to the Fasnacht celebrations.

The flute family

The orchestral flute has its own family. A small version of the flute is called the **piccolo**. It is about half the size of a normal flute. Its high, piercing notes are easily heard above the rest of the **orchestra**. The alto flute and bass flute are larger than the normal flute and play lower notes. They have quiet, mellow sounds. You might see these instruments in the orchestra, but they are more popular in flute **ensembles** and flute choirs.

A worldwide family

The flute is part of a much larger, worldwide family. Flutes come in all shapes and sizes and they have many different names. But all of these instruments are **aerophones**. Their sound is produced when air vibrates.

Nose flutes

Nose flutes are sounded with breath from the player's nose. They are found particularly in the islands of the Pacific Ocean. Many people there believe that breath from the nose is purer than breath from the mouth. In Hawaii, lovers traditionally played nose flutes to send messages at night.

A man in the Sepik region of Papua New Guinea plays a sacred bamboo flute. People in this region believe that the sound of the flute represents the voices of spirits. Women and children are not allowed to play them.

A musician plays the panpipes at a festival in Bolivia, South America. You can see the different lengths of pipe.

Panpipes

A **panpipe** player does not change **pitch** by covering and uncovering holes. Instead, the panpipe has many pipes of different lengths. Every pipe sounds a different pitch – the shorter the pipe, the higher the pitch. The player blows different pipes to change pitch. Panpipes come in many sizes. Groups of panpipers play together in South America and many other places.

Sounds of the gods

In India, the bansuri is a bamboo or wooden flute with six or seven holes. It was believed to be the favourite instrument of a Hindu god, Lord Krishna. Many carvings and paintings show him playing this flute. The sound of Krishna's flute was said to be the most beautiful music on earth.

FLUTE FACTS: Pan and Syrinx

An ancient Greek **myth** tells the story of the god Pan. He fell in love with a beautiful girl called Syrinx. Syrinx did not return Pan's love. She hid herself by turning into a reed by a river. In his disappointment, Pan cut the reed into different lengths. He fastened them together to make the instrument that we now call the panpipes, or syrinx.

What types of music can you play on a flute?

The flute has a gentle, pure sound and is an important member of the **orchestra**. The flute is also played in marching bands, **wind bands**, and flute **ensembles**. Some flautists play **jazz**, **folk**, and pop music. In this kind of music, players use microphones and **amplifiers** to make the soft sound of the flute louder.

Orchestras, wind bands, and flute choirs

You can play the flute on your own or with lots of other people. There are many different groups to choose from. You may have a school orchestra or wind band. There may also be a local flute choir.

Playing in a flute choir is a great way to get to know other flautists.

Wind bands are ensembles which include only wind instruments. Their wide variety of music includes pieces **arranged** or written especially for wind bands. Flute choirs are ensembles made up entirely of flutes. Most flute choirs use the entire family of flutes, from **piccolos** downwards. Larger flutes, such as the contrabass flute, often play the low notes. An even lower flute, the double contrabass or subcontrabass, is more than 5 metres (16 feet) long. It is very rare!

Marching bands

The **fife** is a small flute, usually made from wood or plastic. It has six **tone holes** and no keys. Its shrill notes carry well outdoors. Its high-**pitched** sound, accompanied by drums, has long been used to inspire soldiers on the battlefield. The sight and sound of a marching fife and drum band is thrilling.

 The fife player takes a quick break in a US military marching band.

FLUTE FACTS: Fife bands

In the past, military fife players were boys usually between 10 and 18 years old. Today, both boys and girls can join fife bands. These bands are still very popular in Ireland, the United States, and Canada.

19

Jazz, folk, and pop music

Since the 1950s, the flute's soft notes have been an important sound in the jazz world. Players such as Herbie Mann, Sam Most, and Eric Dolphy made the flute into a popular jazz instrument in the 1960s. They all experimented with getting new and exciting sounds out of the flute. They sang, hummed, and spoke into the flute while playing it.

The sound of the flute in folk music is particularly associated with **Celtic** or Irish bands. The type of flute being played is usually a penny whistle. These flutes are held vertically, like **recorders**. They are made of metal or plastic with six tone holes. These simple whistles are amazingly expressive when played by expert musicians such as Paddy Moloney, Mary Bergin, or Andrea Corr.

The flute was introduced to the world of rock music by the flautist Ian Anderson. He plays with the group Jethro Tull.

Who plays the flute?

Two figures stand out in recent flute history – the French flautist Jean-Pierre Rampal and the Irish flautist James Galway.

Jean-Pierre Rampal (1922–2000) was the first flautist to attract large audiences around the world. He also rediscovered many works for the flute. Every year the Jean-Pierre Rampal competition for flautists is held in Paris.

Sir James Galway (born 1939) is sometimes known as the "man with the golden flute". He often plays a flute made from solid gold. As a child, he learned to play the penny whistle. He played flute in the Berlin Philharmonic **Orchestra** for six years. Then he began his **solo** career. He is well-known for his pop recordings, such as the **soundtracks** for the *Lord of the Rings* movies.

FROM THE EXPERTS

"I do not consider myself as having mastered the flute, but I get a real kick out of trying."

James Galway

Sir James Galway performs with an orchestra in the Barbican Hall, London.

Robert Dick

Robert Dick has been called the "Hendrix of the flute". Like the guitarist Jimi Hendrix, Dick has pushed his instrument to its limits. In his concerts, he uses many different sizes of flute. He also plays using special effects. Sometimes he covers the **blow hole** with his tongue. Other times he blows gently into the flute for a whispering effect. His techniques create a wide range of sounds.

Robert Dick has worked with flute-makers to redesign the instrument. One new feature is the Robert Dick Glissando **Headjoint**. A player can move this headjoint in and out while playing a note. This alters the **pitch** of the note. It produces a sliding effect called "glissando".

This picture shows Robert Dick making a recording with an orchestra. He is playing one of his specially adapted bass flutes.

FROM THE EXPERTS

"Pahud ... never forces the sound either by overworking the instrument or by using a dizzying **vibrato**..."

Gramophone review of Emmanuel Pahud

 The Indian musician Hariprasad Chaurasia (right) performs with Jakir Hussain, a world famous tabla player (the tabla is a type of drum).

Flautists around the world

There are many different types of flute around the world. Many highly skilled players play their own styles of music. In India and beyond, Hariprasad Chaurasia is famous for playing the bansuri (see page 17) – the bamboo flute. The American **jazz** musician Yusef Lateef has experimented with different sounds and styles on the flute. The Italian flautist Nicola Stilo became known for his **bebop** flute style when he played with the American jazz legend Chet Baker. The Canadian **folk** flautist Chris Norman plays a simple wooden flute. Its haunting melodies can be heard on the soundtrack for the film *Titanic*. Classical players such as Emmanuel Pahud and Jeanne Baxtresser are in huge demand. They have played in some of the world's finest orchestras.

How would I learn to play the flute?

The first thing to check is that you are big enough to start playing the flute. You need to be able to hold the flute without straining your neck or hands. If you have trouble, there are special beginner flutes with curved **headjoints** that reduce their overall length. A flute shop or teacher will be able to advise you.

How to find a teacher

Some teachers may visit schools. Others teach at local music centres. Check your local library or music shop for information. If you find a teacher locally, try to learn whether he or she is recommended. In the UK, you could contact the Incorporated Society of Musicians (see page 31). This group lists teachers with recognized professional qualifications and teaching experience.

There are lots of different flutes to choose from. Always ask for advice before buying a flute.

Choosing a flute

Don't just rush out and buy a flute! It's a good idea to borrow or rent a flute to find out whether it's right for you. Some schools have musical instruments that you can borrow or hire. Most music shops have instruments for hire as well.

You can buy a flute at a specialist shop. You should get good advice and a reliable student model there. You can also buy a secondhand flute. Watch for advertisements at school or in your local paper. Whether you choose a new or secondhand flute, try the instrument first. Ask for advice from someone who knows what to look for before buying the flute.

 This CD features some famous flute **solos**.

FLUTE FACTS: Flute birds

With its pure sound and high notes, the flute is very good at pretending to be a bird! Listen for the flute-birds in *Peter and the Wolf* by the Russian composer Sergei Prokofiev and in *The Carnival of the Animals* by the French composer Camille Saint-Saëns.

Putting the flute together

The flute comes in a three parts. Hold each part carefully where there are no keys as you put the flute together.

Twist gently to connect the **middle joint** and **footjoint**. The rod to which the footjoint keys are attached should line up with the middle of the keys on the middle joint.

Twist gently to put the headjoint on. Line up the **blow hole** with the keys.

The flute comes in a hard case. This helps you to carry it around safely when you are not using it.

Looking after the flute – dos and don'ts

- Don't leave your flute near a radiator, even in its case. Extreme temperatures are not good for it.

- Do warm your flute up before playing by blowing gently into it.

- Do always dry the inside of your flute after playing. You will find a cleaning stick in your case. Thread a clean cotton cloth through the eye at the end. Push the stick through each joint separately. Be gentle when cleaning the headjoint.

- Do clean fingermarks off the outside with a lint-free cloth.

- Don't fiddle with the screws, springs, or crown! Ask your teacher for help.

Enjoy yourself!

Once you have an instrument and a teacher, it's time to start playing. You will probably need to learn to read music. You should also try to practise regularly. A little practice every day is better than trying to catch up in one long practice! Soon you will be learning scales and playing your first pieces. The most important thing is to enjoy playing your flute!

Your teacher will give you exercises and pieces to practise. Try to do a little practice each day!

Recordings to listen to

Selection from the classical repertoire

Pieces

Bach, J.S., Sonatas

Copland, Aaron, *Duo for Flute and Piano*

Fauré, Gabriel, *Fantasie*

Handel, G.F., Sonatas

Hindemith, Paul, Sonata

Honegger, Arthur, *Danse de la Chèvre*

Ibert, Jacques, Concerto

Messiaen, Olivier, *Le Merle Noir*

Mozart, W. A., Flute Concertos, K. 313, K. 314

Nielsen, Carl, Concerto

Poulenc, Francis, Sonata

Prokofiev, Sergei, Sonata

Telemann, Georg, Suite in A Minor

Recordings

Galway, James, *The Very Best of James Galway* (BMG), *Wings of Song* (Deutsche Grammophon, 2004)

Rampal, Jean-Pierre, *Master of the Flute* (Fabulous, 2005)

Jazz/folk/pop/world flute recordings

Anderson, Ian (flautist with Jethro Tull), *Rupi's Dance* (R&M, 2003)

Chaurasia, Hariprasad, *Flying Beyond: Improvisations on Bamboo Flute* (Eternal Music, 1995)

Dick, Robert, *Jazz Standards on Mars* (Enja, 2003), *Third Stone from the Sun* (New World, 1994)

Dolphy, Eric, *Out to Lunch* (Blue Note, 1999)

Lateef, Yusef, *Live at Pep's* (Impulse, 1993), *The Golden Flute* (Verve, 2004)

Mann, Herbie, *Celebration* (Lightyear, 1997), *Opalescence* (Kokopelli, 1994)

Moloney, Paddy (leader of the Irish band The Chieftains), *Tin Whistles* (Claddagh, 2000)

Timeline of flute history

50,000 BC   Earliest known flute found in Slovenia

900s   Earliest pictures of the **transverse** flute in the West

1300s   The flute is used as a military instrument, together with the drums

1500s   The flute is made in three standard sizes – alto, tenor, and bass – and played in groups called consorts

1700s   The flute starts to become a popular **solo** instrument

1707   French flautist Jacques Hotteterre (1674–1763) publishes the first flute method book to teach the basics of flute-playing

1741   One of the first professional flautists, Johann Joachim Quantz (1697–1773), enters the service of Frederick the Great of Prussia (1712–86). He composes hundreds of pieces of flute music for the king.

1750s   The flute becomes a regular member of the classical symphony **orchestra**

1832   After hearing Nicholson playing, Theobald Boehm (1794–1881) invents a new flute design

1847   Boehm makes the first metal flute

1900   Boehm flutes become the most commonly played types of flute in the West

1950s   Beginning of serious presence in **jazz** music for the flute

1960s   British flute-maker Albert Cooper makes innovations to the standard Boehm flute. These are quickly adopted by flute manufacturers.

1975   James Galway starts his solo career

1992   Jean-Pierre Rampal celebrates his 70th birthday with a concert at Avery Fisher Hall in New York

late 20th century   Flute makers such as Eva Kingma and Brannen Brothers develop new types of flute

Glossary

aerophone instrument that produces its sound through the vibration of a body of air

amplifier piece of equipment that makes a sound louder

arranged adapted from its original version

bebop type of jazz that features fast improvisation

blow hole hole in the lip plate of the flute through which the player blows

Celtic describing the culture and traditions of the Celts, a people originally from Scotland, Ireland, and southwest England

embouchure shape made by your lips to produce a steady stream of air

ensemble group

fife small flute made from wood or plastic, usually played in marching bands

folk music of the people

footjoint bottom section of the flute

headjoint top section of the flute that includes the lip plate

jazz type of music that developed in the 20th century in the United States

middle joint middle section of the flute that has most of the keys

moral to do with good or bad behaviour

myth ancient story

orchestra large musical group made up of many different instruments

panpipe instrument made with different length pipes, played by blowing across the top of each pipe in turn

piccolo member of the flute family, about half the size of the normal flute

pitch high or low sound of a note

porcelain type of very fine clay

recorder type of flute that is held straight down and blown through a mouthpiece called a fipple

reed small, fine piece of cane which vibrates when air is blown across it

solo performed alone

soundtrack music for a film

tone hole hole in a musical instrument that can be covered and uncovered to change the pitch

transverse played or held sideways

vibration movement to and fro

vibrato slight changes up and down in the pitch of a note, made by the player's breath or by the movement of the player's hand on a stringed instrument

wind band instrumental group made up of woodwind instruments

woodwind instrument played by blowing and originally made from wood. The four usual woodwind instruments of the orchestra are the flute, oboe, clarinet, and bassoon.

Further resources

Books

Abracadabra Flute Duets, Malcolm Pollock (A&C Black, 1992)

Abracadabra Flute: The Way to Learn Through Songs and Tunes, Malcolm Pollock, (A&C Black, 2001)

Usborne Book of Easy Flute Tunes, Katie Elliott and Emma Danes (Usborne, 2000)

Young Musicians: Playing the Flute, Recorder, and other Woodwind, Simon Walton (Watts, 2003)

Websites

http://www.flutewise.com/fw/index.html
Website for Flutewise aimed at young players everywhere. You can subscribe to the quarterly Flutewise magazine and attend Flutewise events.

http://www.ism.org/registers.php
The Incorporated Society of Musicians has a list of registered flute teachers.

http://www.bfs.org.uk/
Website for the British Flute Society.

http://www.bigwhistle.co.uk/index.asp
Everything you need to know about the penny whistle.

http://www.flute.com/
Excellent resource for flute enthusiasts.

Index

Titles in the *Learning Musical Instruments* series include:

Hardback 978 0 431 057835

Hardback 978 0 431 057842

Hardback 978 0 431 057859

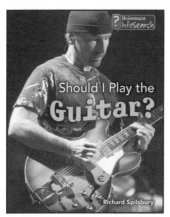

Hardback 978 0 431 057866

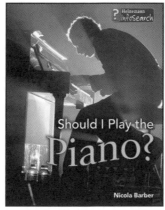

Hardback 978 0 431 057873

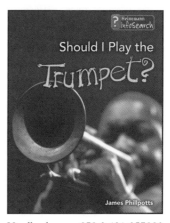

Hardback 978 0 431 057880

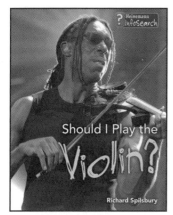

Hardback 978 0 431 057897

Find out about other titles from Heinemann Library on our website www.heinemann.co.uk/library